The Horse's Haiku

First edition 2018

Library of Congress Catalog Card Number pending
ISBN 978-0-7636-8916-2

17 18 19 20 21 22 TLF 10 9 8 7 6 5 4 3 2 1

Printed in Dongguan, Guangdong, China

This book was typeset in Filosophia.
The illustrations were done in watercolor.

Candlewick Press
99 Dover Street
Somerville, Massachusetts 02144

visit us at www.candlewick.com

The Horse's Haiku

Michael J. Rosen

illustrated by
Stan Fellows

CANDLEWICK PRESS

In the Field

dappled gray mare stoops
to graze, the dappled gray dawn
her saddle blanket

wobbling hours-old foal,
your limbs can't guess at the grace
and gaits that await

one foal nods, slicing
the fog of shared breaths—the mare
nods in agreement

wriggling in the dirt,
dust cloud of kicking hooves, then—
poof!—horse standing there

cloudy-day pond: now
horse and shadow become horse
and reflection — now . . .

four pause in a pool
of rainwater, then a fifth
dips groundward and drinks

under one willow
horses huddle—half shaded,
half casting shadows

snowfall whitens all
but two darks: unfrozen stream
and horses huddled

frozen hoofprints stamp
into the fossil record
of February

hooves hinged together:
white-and-black stallion and his
hail-dappled shadow

At the Barn

winter dawn's wan glow . . .
from each stall door, vapor clouds
answer your boot steps

pausing to flatten
your fingers before horse teeth
seize the apple slice

above the fence rails
felt-soft muzzle, snuffled puffs—
lips flutter your palm

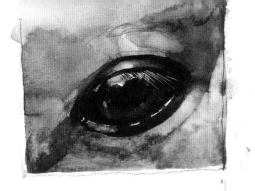

standing eye to eye,
that's you—your world—mirrored where
horse sees side to side

above the muffled
clip-clop of dry hooves, the rain's
first pitter-patter

outside the barn door:
pooled storm water—when the wind
stops, horses appear

cattle dog below

filly's arched belly: four legs

resting among four

lifting his head high
how much water dribbles back
into the bucket

the wither's quick twitch
flicks off the biting horsefly
but just this instant

dozing familiars:
mare settled in her stall, cat
balanced on her rump

napping, open-eyed . . .
pinto's cocked hind leg dithers
on a toe's curved edge

Under Saddle

front leg half-folded
horse's hoof rests in your palm
weightless as prayer

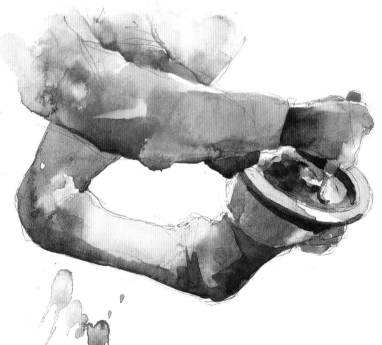

right foot slid in place,
heels pressed down in both stirrups—
trust is your seat belt

through the horse's sights—
one forward ear, one backward—
there, you see your ride

that sweet instant when
trotting's bounce and rumble smooths
into canter's glide

daybreak, low tide—flash
of sunbeams between saddle
and posting rider

half a ton plus you—
four exaggerated grins
bear all that burden

plank-bridge marimba—
hooves plunk the same damped rhythm,
heading out and back

the pokiest horse
with the new rider's loose reins
first back to the barn

time, too, must stretch as
rear hooves launch from earth . . . and then
front hooves ground again

cupped hand's clap against
wet chest—such loud gratitude
after the day's ride

it still surprises! —
that steaming heat loosed beneath
the saddle, uncinched!

dismounting today
tomorrow already slipped
one foot in stirrups

GRAZING: A NOTE ON THE HAIKU

horse champs another
clump of grass . . . munching . . . chewing —
like this haiku!*

I've come to think of writing haiku as a form of grazing.

Horses are grazers: they continually eat in the same area before moving on to the next. (Creatures who are browsers, by contrast, move around, eating a little of this, a little of that.) So, too, the art of haiku is standing right here, seizing a fleeting observation, and then mulling words over and over until a poem emerges.

Horses are prey animals. With eyes on the sides of their face, the collective alertness of their herd's senses, and the ability to sleep standing up in case danger requires them to flee, horses are finely tuned to the noises, scents, and motions in their environment.

Similarly, I've come to see haiku as an act of vigilance.

Vigilant grazing: Haiku is the practice of seeing still. (Yes, think "sitting still," but applied to the mind and senses.) So while such sustained attention might pertain to many forms of writing, what's unique to haiku is that there's no browsing onto something else. Each poem stays here and now. The challenge is finding words to suspend one instant of awareness within a poem's sparse lines.

Basho, the Japanese writer who inspired much of what we know about this poetic form, said that a haiku lives on the tip of the tongue. *It's . . . it's, you know. Wait, I've almost got it!* The right words are . . . but then they aren't! So a haiku requires you, a reader, to recognize what's being suggested. Seen in that light, haiku is an interaction between a writer and a reader. Through a shared language, both experience a particular moment. A similar interaction exists between a rider and a horse: they share a language — their immediate circumstances, their history of practice, their knowledge of each other — that permits this profound partnership.

---

* While you probably hear the word *haiku* as two syllables, in Japanese, each vowel has a distinct sound: "ha-i-ku."